LAW AND POLITICS

LAW & POLITICS

BY

THE RIGHT HON.
LORD MACMILLAN
LL.D.

THE HENRY SIDGWICK MEMORIAL LECTURE
DELIVERED AT NEWNHAM COLLEGE
CAMBRIDGE
9 NOVEMBER 1935

CAMBRIDGE
AT THE UNIVERSITY PRESS
1935

CAMBRIDGE
UNIVERSITY PRESS

University Printing House, Cambridge CB2 8BS, United Kingdom

Published in the United States of America by Cambridge University Press, New York

Cambridge University Press is part of the University of Cambridge.

It furthers the University's mission by disseminating knowledge in the pursuit of education, learning and research at the highest international levels of excellence.

www.cambridge.org
Information on this title: www.cambridge.org/9781107671102

© Cambridge University Press 1935

First published 1935
Re-issued 2014

A catalogue record for this publication is available from the British Library

ISBN 978-1-107-67110-2 Paperback

LAW AND POLITICS

There is much to commend the institution of an annual namesake Lecture as a means of keeping fresh among us the memory of our departed masters. It ensures that each year one person at least, the chosen lecturer, shall give some thought to the life and work of the great man under whose auspices he is to speak; and his audience, too, if he is fortunate enough to have one, will for a passing hour recall the merits of him who is gone if only to compare them with the shortcomings of the speaker on whom his nominal mantle has fallen. Many such memorials have been founded in our Universities but in no instance more fittingly than in that of Henry Sidgwick, for it was in the lecture room that his incomparable gift of exposition found its most congenial atmosphere. In his case the appropriateness of this annual commemoration is enhanced by its association with Newnham College, itself an imperishable monument to his chivalrous crusade and under whose roof he spent the last and happiest years of his life.

Already the generation which knew Sidgwick has passed away in the thirty-five years which have elapsed since his death. The lecturer of to-day belongs to the next generation. But as in pious duty bound I have not failed to read the admirable Memoir of his life which we owe to his brother and his wife. I read it not only in order to be able to picture what manner of man he was, as he appeared to those who knew him best, but also in order to recapture, if I could, the intellectual mood of his day, to appreciate the nature of the problems which then confronted the thinker, and to estimate the measure of success which he achieved in their solution.

Fortunately we have still with us one of those who knew Sidgwick intimately. In his altogether delightful volume of reminiscences entitled *For my Grandson*, Sir Frederick Pollock tells us that "Henry Sidgwick was a born philosopher, ardent in the pursuit of truth, capable of sacrificing worldly advantage to his conscience, yet always judicious and abhorring dogmatism to the point of enjoying suspense of judgment for its own sake. . . . In speculation he was sceptical, in action cautious but not timid." In a later passage he says of Sidgwick and Jackson, whom he describes as "the leading captains of modern and ancient philosophy" during his residence at Cambridge, that "they taught younger men to seek for themselves and to seek with an exacting conscience". And then he adds these words, so characteristic of the learned expositor of Spinoza: "Even if you consider philosophy merely as an intellectual game, there is no fun in playing with people (including yourself) who fudge their conclusions."

This is the testimony of one who saw and heard Sidgwick. But we, who are unhappily confined to the written record, can well confirm it, for it is just this spirit of conscientious candour and courageous diffidence which is exhaled not only from his more intimate diaries and letters but also from his published writings. In describing, in a moment of self-examination at the age of twenty-six "that particular aggregate of psychological phenomena" which he called himself, he exclaimed: "For my part, I have determined to love the Ideal only." To that dedication of his spirit he remained true to his last breath.

Now it may seem more than a little odd after this preamble that in choosing a topic for this year's lecture I should have selected a subject so arid and so apparently alien to Sidgwick's genius as *Law and Politics*. What right have lawyers and politicians, those noisy and mercenary persons, to invade these quiet cloisters? But in truth I have ample justification, for Sidgwick all his days was intensely preoccupied with this very theme of my choice, as those can best testify who, like myself, have studied his great work on *The Science of Politics*, that "heavy book" as he not unjustly characterises it. Let there be no mistake, however. I do not use the word "politics" in the sense in which it is so often used by chairmen of public meetings who reassure their audiences by informing them that the cause they are met to promote has nothing to do with politics. It is remarkable, by the way, how invariably this announcement is greeted with applause when one reflects how vitally the happiness and prosperity of everyone of us are concerned in the conduct of our government. But of course the disclaimer is always understood to refer to party politics in the sinister and derogatory sense of that expression and this aspect of politics, which Sidgwick once described as a "blind free fight", was as distasteful to him as it would be out of place for a person in my judicial position to discuss it.

No. What interested Sidgwick supremely, and what must always be of interest to every thinking citizen, was politics in the sense of the science of associated humanity. He was essentially a moral, rather than a metaphysical philosopher. Hence he treated politics as a branch, indeed as the main branch, of ethics. There are no doubt problems of ethics which affect the individual and the individual only and which would exercise the mind of the solitary denizen of a desert island in the conduct of his daily life. But most of the problems of ethics, and certainly the most vexed ones, concern our relations with our fellow men. Few of the moral virtues could be practised by us if there were no other human beings towards whom they could be exhibited.

It is easy to see the pathway by which Sidgwick was led from ethics to politics. Most of us have traversed it, though some of us in the opposite direction. For politics in the scientific sense is the art of organising and managing human beings in the associations into which they are brought by their common membership of a city, a nation, or some larger social unit. This art, inasmuch as it has to deal with human beings endowed with moral consciences, cannot confine itself merely to economic or disciplinary regulations. It must ultimately concern itself with the fundamental considerations of ethics.

The very first sentence of Aristotle's *Politics* takes one at once into the moral sphere. "Seeing", he says, "that every State is a sort of association and every association is formed for the attainment of some Good—for some presumed Good is the end of all action—it is evident that as some Good is the object of all associations, so in the highest degree is the supreme Good the object of that association which is supreme and embraces all the rest, in other words of the State or political association." Observe that the word "Good", the key word of ethics, occurs no less than four times in that opening paragraph.

Thus the moral philosopher sooner or later cannot escape from the consideration of political science. The human being who is the subject of his study is a social being, whose activities for good or for evil are in large measure determined for him by the society in which he lives, and that society in turn derives its character from its political constitution. True, politics may be said to deal rather with the setting than with the substance of the moral life, with the conditions under which the citizen lives rather than with the ethical quality of his individual life. But the interaction between the citizen and the political medium in which he lives is so close and constant as to affect his moral nature profoundly. And so the moral philosopher finds himself discussing politics—in their ethical aspect, no doubt, but with a full appreciation of the truth that the extent to which the individual can attain the ideal of the moral life is deeply affected by the character of the social organisation, in other words, of the political system, under which he lives. It is difficult, as Sidgwick indicates, to sort out the elements in social life which may properly be called political because they are so intimately combined with the other elements. Still, it is possible to make at least a theoretical analysis of our social life and to isolate for special study its political components.

What Sidgwick sought was to give precision to our political concepts as a contribution to the art of moral government, and he defined the scope of his study as being "concerned primarily with constructing, on the basis of certain psychological premises, the system of relations which ought to be established among the persons governing, and between them and the governed, in a society composed of civilised men as we know them". While not a few of the questions to which he addressed himself in pursuing this study now seem to us somewhat dimmed by the distance which we have so swiftly travelled since his day, Sidgwick's discussion of the proper functions of Government remains still full of instruction and guidance for us. To his treatment of this topic Professor Marshall paid the tribute of saying that it was admitted to be by far the best thing in any language. For us to-day it has a special value for it furnishes us with the wisdom of a singularly balanced mind on what has become the cardinal problem of political science, which when Sidgwick wrote was already beginning to come into prominence; I mean the conflict which has since grown so acute between Individualism and State Socialism—to use his own terms—as rival theories of civil government. The economic doctrine of *laissez-faire*, the doctrine that enlightened self-interest if left to itself best conduces to the social well-being of the community, had held sway in this country since the time of Adam Smith and was still cherished by many adherents of one of the great political parties with almost religious fervour. With them it was a far greater achievement to secure the repeal than to secure the enactment of a statute. But already there were ominous signs of change and presumptuous hands were already being laid on the ark of the covenant. "It is universally recognised", says Sidgwick, "that the present drift of opinion and practice is in the direction of increasing the range and volume of the interferences of government in the affairs of individuals." So he wrote some forty years ago. I wonder what would have been his comment on our legislation of the past two decades! In the ninety-second chapter of his great work on the American Commonwealth Bryce describes the inception of a similar process in the United States. More and more the main issue in political science has come to be—not whether the State should intervene at all in the regulation of our daily lives but where the frontier line ought most wisely to be drawn between the province of State activity and that of individual enterprise. On all hands it is now recognised that the policy of *laissez-faire* which gave us no doubt our industrial and commercial supremacy but also gave us our slums and many other attendant evils, must give place to a new regime. The contest has now shifted to a new ground on which those who are all for State regimentation do battle with those who defend what they regard as the rightful strongholds of individual initiative. The definition of the sphere of government has become the main preoccupation of the student of political science. We have travelled far since Tom Paine—that early champion of the people's rights—proclaimed that "The more perfect civilisation is, the less occasion has it for government...it is but few general laws that civilised life requires".

This changed attitude of mind has come about not only through a revulsion from the old theory and its attendant evils, but also as a consequence of the increased complexity of modern life. Politics are concerned with the regulation of the contacts of human beings with each other and the enormous changes which have come about in the mechanism of life have infinitely increased these contacts and consequently the necessity for their regulation. Let me quote side by side a passage from Sidgwick's *Science of Politics* and one from the Archbishop of York's broadcast lecture on "Faith and Freedom" on 30th May last. "It is easy", says Sidgwick, "to see how new occasions for this kind of interference may continually arise: either because the mischief in question has been increased or newly introduced through the closer massing and more complicated relations of human beings which the development of industry and civilisation brings with it; or because mischiefs of long standing have been unveiled by the increased insight of advancing science, or possible remedies hitherto unknown have been pointed out." In my parallel passage from the Archbishop, His Grace declares that "with the development of centralisation which the new means of communication have made possible and the growth of planning which mass-production has made necessary it has been natural that the State should invade spheres hitherto left to voluntary effort".

The same insight which enabled Sidgwick to discover this new movement of political thought enabled him also to perceive its dangers. He recognised that a crowded world cannot safely be left to its own devices and that in such a world a certain amount of what we now term social legislation is essential to the preservation of the liberty of the individual.

Such measures, he saw, may promote rather than diminish freedom. This is essentially true. I am not less but more the captain of my soul in a city which is well sewered, well paved, well policed, and free from slums and the diseases they breed, and in which the education, the health and the welfare of my fellow citizens are promoted by sensible measures.

But the defect of all social policies, as Sidgwick saw, is their tendency to run to extremes, and now we hear on all sides a warning that if we do not take heed we may wake up some fine morning to find all our liberties gone, overwhelmed by a mass of legislation which by depriving life of all its individual initiative will rob it of all its happiness and interest. Just as the unrestrained policy of *laissez-faire* wrought many evils which we are now slowly redressing with much cost and labour, so there is a risk that the opposite policy may in turn bring in its train no less, though different, evils, if not vigorously guarded.

That serious alarm as to the present trend of political thought is entertained in many quarters is manifest, and the danger which is threatened is danger to our liberties. "Freedom, our traditional treasure, is threatened," says the Archbishop of York, "how can it be saved?" Before me as I write lie the writings of four authors, nurtured in very different pastures, who have discerned the same impending menace. First I open a book which hails from the land of the free entitled *The Challenge to Liberty*. There I find ex-President Hoover impelled to vindicate the cause of liberty in his country with almost passionate eloquence against the encroachments of regimentation. His opening words are: "For the first time in two generations the American people are faced with the primary issue of humanity and all Government—the issue of human liberty." No less trenchant language is employed elsewhere by my friend the President of Columbia University. But Europe is evidently in no better case, for here is General Smuts, in his Rectorial Address on "Freedom" at St Andrews University, telling us that: "In many if not most European countries the standard of human freedom has already fallen far below that of the nineteenth century. Perhaps I do not exaggerate when I say that of what we call liberty in its full human meaning—freedom of thought, speech, action, self-expression—there is to-day less than there has been during the last two thousand years." Let us come nearer home. The third of my books is entitled *The New Despotism*, and here I find the Lord Chief Justice of England once more buckling on the armour of Sir Edward Coke and, in the sacred cause of the Rule of Law, offering battle to that ancient foe of freedom—the executive. And finally in one of the last of his public utterances, when at the Royal Institution last April he traced the history of *Liberty under the Common Law*, my lamented colleague Lord Tomlin, with the studious moderation which characterises the utterances of Lords of Appeal, permitted himself "a sigh over the ever increasing tendency, due perhaps to the ever increasing complexity of modern life, to limit in so many fields the freedom of action of the individual" and ventured still "to proclaim the importance above all else of the freedom of the mind, to recall that through the history of our law's development...there runs a romantic thread of passionate attachment to freedom of thought and speech and to maintain that only when that freedom is accorded and in the atmosphere created by it, can the mind of man develop and display its finest flowers". Such quotations from such responsible leaders of thought in very diverse spheres—and I could multiply them indefinitely—plainly indicate that something is amiss.

There are many diagnoses of the mischief and indeed the causes are manifold. But there is one which to my mind is plainly among those at work, and it brings me at last to the special topic with which I have promised to deal—the relation of law and politics.

In a limited sense law may be said to be merely the vehicle of politics, for it is by legislation that the politician gives expression and effect to his policy—at least in countries which enjoy—perhaps I should rather say possess—representative government. The statute book reflects in its contents the prevalent political theories of the time. No one can study its recent volumes without being struck by the extent to which they are nowadays almost monopolised by immense masses of elaborate social legislation. And the counterpart of this is the growth of our annual expenditure on these social activities in England and Wales from 31 millions to 430 millions in the course of the last thirty years or so, an expenditure which is still rising. Our country is not alone in this new development of legislative activity. I have a volume of nearly nine hundred pages in which the Labour Office at Geneva published in 1933 the results of its International Survey of Social Services, covering twenty-three other countries as well as our own.

But while Law in the sense of legislation is merely a means of enforcing policy, there is another sense in which law is, or ought to be, the master of policy. Law is something much greater and nobler than the contents of any statute book, of any code, of any volume of judicial decisions. It is the guardian and vindicator of the two most precious things in the world—justice and liberty. It may well be that at any particular time its manifestations in the governance of our daily lives may fall lamentably short of attaining its ideals. It may

even be perverted, for it is an instrument confided to fallible, it may even be to wicked,
human agencies. But its ideal remains constant
and unchanging. By the standards of justice
and liberty which it sets up all governments, all
political theories, must ultimately be judged
and must ultimately stand or fall.

It should then be the aim of the science of
politics to devise, and of the art of politics to
promote, such a system of government as will
ensure the fullest enjoyment of justice and
liberty by all who come within its scope.
"I suppose", says Dean Inge, "politics con-
sists in choosing always the second-best."
I should be sorry to subscribe to this depressing
doctrine, though I should equally be the first
to admit that in an imperfect world the perfect
ideal is not attainable. But to cease to strive for
the best and to decline in disillusioned lethargy
on the second-best is in the statesman the
unpardonable sin.

Let us examine a little more closely these
great conceptions of justice and liberty. In
political science justice may be said to have a
rather wider significance than in its ordinary

legal application. To the lawyer the essence of justice is that the law shall be the same for all, that it shall be administered without fear or favour and that it shall secure for each citizen that to which by the law of the land he is justly entitled. But the student of political science asks the more fundamental question—is the law itself just? And here he enters upon much more difficult and controversial ground. For while all would have the laws to be just, there are almost infinite variations in the conception of what is just—every citizen has his own idea about it. Nor is there any absolute standard of justice. The idea of justice which each one of us entertains is affected by our training, by our economic position, by our sentiments, by our prejudices. What may seem just to one man in one age may seem to another man in another age the very quintessence of injustice. The historian can supply us with any number of political measures which at the time were conceived and honestly conceived by their promoters to be just but which now outrage our sense of justice. Yet there is in every age a public conscience which according to its lights is alive to particular injustices, even if it cannot define justice in the abstract, and the efficiency of a government is judged by its success in removing these. Each age seems to have its own problem. At one time it is the injustice of slavery, at another the injustice of woman's position, which awakens the nation's conscience. At present I should say that the kind of injustice which most exercises the world is economic injustice.

It follows from this constant expansion, I hope I may say progress, in our conception of justice that the law which is the framework of our social structure can never be static. "Respect for the law", a present-day writer has said, "depends in the long run on the power to change it." But there will always be a lag in the process of change, for the law cannot be altered without careful consideration. There is a principle of justice itself which forbids inconsiderate change in response to gusts of public sentiment, for the people of a country arrange their lives and their affairs in reliance on the stability of the law, and every change in the law involves a certain amount of disturbance and often even some injustice. So it is the part of the wise politician to weigh well the measures for the alteration of the law which he is urged to undertake in the interests of justice, lest his well-meant efforts may work an injustice greater than that which he has set out to cure. He was a wise statesman who said: "Where it is not necessary to change it is necessary not to change."

Here I may venture to emphasise a distinction which is apt to be lost sight of in these days; I mean the distinction between justice and philanthropy. Justice requires that each man shall receive his deserts, the reward of his merits and the penalties of his demerits. "Whatsoever a man soweth, that shall he also reap", says St Paul. There are those who find this a hard doctrine and who would destroy the whole relation between merit and reward on which our moral as well as our legal system is based. Herbert Spencer discerned the beginnings of this mood over forty years ago when he said that "daily legislation betrays little anxiety that each shall have what belongs to him but great anxiety that he shall have that which belongs to somebody else". Where social justice finds its true sphere is in securing that each shall have a fair and equal chance of winning the rewards of life. Justice may equalise the opportunities of life but it cannot equalise the ability to take advantage of these opportunities. It has been suggested that material things might be divided equally and shared equally in common, leaving special merit to find its reward in immaterial things, such as fame and public approval, but there may be and often is as much injustice, and consequent ill feeling, over the distribution of intangible as over the distribution of tangible rewards. However, I am not considering how ideal justice would re-shape the world. I am trying to think out how law may best serve the cause of social justice in the world as we find it; and I suggest that a good working test is that such measures as tend to remove unfair and man-made handicaps and to promote equality of opportunity for all may be deemed to be just measures; while those which tend to deprive of adequate reward those who have displayed merit in using the opportunities afforded to them are unjust measures. An acute commentator has observed that we are "confronted with the paradox that man is at once a social being and therefore co-operative, and an individual personality and therefore competitive". We cannot eliminate this duality and so we come back to the central problem of where the line should be drawn between co-operation whose rewards are shared, and competition whose rewards are monopolised. But I am getting perilously near controversial topics.

I have bracketed justice and liberty as the supreme ends which the spirit of law prescribes for political science. In truth, however, justice and liberty are not and cannot be isolated from each other, for there can be no real justice without liberty, no real liberty without justice. A much graver wrong is done to a man in unjustly depriving him of his liberty of action, of thought or of speech, than in unjustly depriving him of his material possessions. The supreme injustice is the coercion of the soul. The history of civil government in this country has been the history of the slow but sure achievement of civil liberty for its citizens, and it is because in other less happy lands around us we see liberty being not only threatened but destroyed that we must take heed that this menace does not reach our shores.

Now it is by the law that our liberty is assured. "To be free", said Lord Mansfield, "is to live under a government by law." The badge of servitude is subjection to the arbitrary will of another and the law is the sworn foe of arbitrariness. The first of the direct guarantees of civil liberty in this country, is "the open administration of justice according to known laws truly interpreted and fair constructions of evidence." These are the words of Hallam in his *Constitutional History*, as quoted by Lord Justice Farwell in a famous case. That the law shall be certain and the same for all, that no person shall be deprived of his liberty save by due process of law, that all charges must be founded upon and formulated in accordance with existing law, that the prosecutor must prove his case by competent evidence, that the accused must have every opportunity of defending himself and that the trial must be conducted by an independent and impartial judge and, not least important, that the accused can only be detained on a definite charge and must be brought to trial within a definite time—these are the bulwarks of liberty—and so, as Heraclitus said five hundred years before Christ: "The people ought to fight in defence of the law as they do of their city wall."

But this hard-won liberty which the law assures to us is ever at the mercy of politics. Where the political system of a country breaks down, as it has broken down in several of the great countries of Europe, then the rule of law, which needs a sound political structure for its support, collapses in turn and there is substituted for it that horrid arbitrariness which is the negation of law and of which we have had such painful examples of late. Thus it is true that law and politics are indissolubly linked together. The government of a state must be based on sound theories of political science or at any moment it may be overthrown and anarchy or tyranny take its place, and in its downfall justice and liberty alike will perish. What particular form of government will best ensure the preservation of these essential rights it is the province of the political scientist to discuss. Probably it will vary in its constitution according to the stage of progress which the nation has reached and according to the genius of its people. But the fact that in this country of ours, almost alone in the world, freedom still survives undiminished may justify us in maintaining that its best safeguard for us at any rate is the democratic system of representative government which we have devised for ourselves. It has a theoretical as well as a practical justification. Liberty is not licence and it can only be enjoyed in obedience to laws which involve some restrictions of individual freedom of action. But if these restrictions are imposed by our own choice and can be altered by our own will they lose their irksomeness. No one will be bold enough to say that a representative democracy is the final product of political wisdom, but it at least has the merit of giving effect to the will of the majority of the people and thus of ensuring that only such limitations on liberty shall be imposed as the majority are willing to accept in the general interest. Professor Whitehead reminds us that "a doctrine as to the social mingling of liberty and compulsion is required. A mere unqualified demand for liberty is the issue of shallow philosophy, equally noxious with the antithetical cry for mere conformation to standard pattern." The task which is common to law and to politics, each in its own province, is so to reconcile the freedom which is necessary if the individual is to give of his best to mankind with the compulsion which is necessary if the community is to exist in which alone he can enjoy his freedom.

When so much depends for all of us on the due discharge of their duty by our lawyers and our politicians to whom we have confided the guardianship of those precious treasures—justice and liberty—are we quite just in so constantly deriding their character and their activities? I am not going to indulge in platitudes about the quality of British justice and it would hardly be seemly for me to vindicate the merits of the profession to which I belong. But I may bespeak a more charitable, a more appreciative—I will say, a more just—attitude to those who devote their lives to politics. Perhaps the politicians are themselves in no small measure responsible for the distrust which they so often incur, for far too large a part of their energy is spent in abuse of each other. If you think of it, it seems a strange and ironical arrangement that when the country has entrusted to a particular group of men the arduous and delicate task of conducting the business of the nation, we at the same time expect and permit them to be harassed by every form of obstruction and vituperation. It is as if we had employed a surgeon to perform a difficult operation and then had arranged that his elbow should be jogged at the most critical moments.

You have probably all read F. S. Oliver's Political Testament in the third volume of *The Endless Adventure* published after his death. "The hardest chapter to write about Politicians", he says, "is that which deals with their morals." But his next words are: "Let me say again what I said at the beginning—that in my view 'politics is the noblest career that any man can choose...'. Stout must be the hearts of those who take so great a risk and who dedicate themselves—souls as well as bodies—to the service of their country." And then he quotes Montaigne, than whom, as he justly says, few if any writers have been freer from illusions: "I am of opinion", says that sage, "that the most honourable calling is to serve the Public and to be useful to the many." When so much is at stake in these days I think then that we might be a little more generous in our criticisms of those upon whom we place the burden of decisions which we shirk ourselves. We are more likely to get good work from our politicians if we expect good work from them, for praise and confidence are much better stimulants to wise effort than abuse and mistrust. Fair criticism is another matter. I hope we shall always have that.

I cannot say that I conclude this lecture with much satisfaction, for I have an uncomfortable feeling that I have stirred far more questions than I have answered. I suppose this must always be the case when one seeks to explore fundamental principles. Indeed I doubt if any fundamental principles are susceptible of precise formulation. At any rate none of the doctors and sages whom, not only in my youth, I have eagerly frequented has expounded any social theory to my complete satisfaction. I console myself, however, with the reflection that in my avoidance of dogma I have perhaps proved myself for a brief hour a not unworthy disciple of Sidgwick, that least dogmatic of philosophers.

After all, the things that matter most are always the most elusive. They derive from instinct rather than from reason. So I shall resort to a poet, and not to either a lawyer or a politician, for the noblest expression of that ideal which is the aspiration alike of law and politics. It is four hundred years since the words were written, but never has there been better cause to realise their truth than in these days:

> "Ah! freedom is a noble thing;
> Freedom makes man to have liking,
> Freedom all solace to man gives,
> He lives at ease that freely lives."

www.ingramcontent.com/pod-product-compliance
Ingram Content Group UK Ltd.
Pitfield, Milton Keynes, MK11 3LW, UK
UKHW042141280225
455719UK00001B/21